WITHDRAWN
HARVARD LIBRARY
WITHDRAWN

What Is FREEDOM OF CHOICE?

Harry Settanni

UNIVERSITY
PRESS OF
AMERICA

What Is FREEDOM OF CHOICE?

Harry Settanni, Ph.D.

UNIVERSITY
PRESS OF
AMERICA

Lanham • New York • London

Copyright © 1992 by
University Press of America®, Inc.
4720 Boston Way
Lanham, Maryland 20706

3 Henrietta Street
London WC2E 8LU England

All rights reserved
Printed in the United States of America
British Cataloging in Publication Information Available

Library of Congress Cataloging-in-Publication Data
Settanni, Harry, 1945–
What is freedom of choice? / by Harry Settanni.
p. cm.
Includes bibliographical references.
1. Free will and determinism. I. Title.
BJ1461.S53   1992   123'.5—dc20   92–12397 CIP

ISBN 0–8191–8674–0 (pbk. : alk. paper)

BJ
1461
.S53
1992

The paper used in this publication meets the minimum requirements of American National Standard for Information Sciences—Permanence of Paper for Printed Library Materials, ANSI Z39.48–1984.

Contents

Acknowledgments

Chapters
I. THE PROBLEM OF FREE CHOICE 1
   A. Free Choice and Science 1
      i. The Christian Tradition 1
      ii. Augustine 2
      iii. The Enlightenment 3
      iv. Determinism for Spinoza and Hobbes 3
      v. Science vs. Religion 3
   B. The Problem for Kant 3
      i. Pietistic Training in Gymnasium 4
      ii. Enlightenment Training in University 4
      iii. Either Science or Religion 4
      iv. Why not Reconciliation? 4
      v. Contradictions 4

II. ONE POSSIBLE SOLUTION: COMPATIBILISM 7
   A. Aristotle 7
      i. Knowledge and Action 8
         a. Knowing the Good 8
         b. Doing it 8
      ii. Major and Minor Premises 9
         a. The Major Premise 9
         b. The Minor Premise 9
   B. Spinoza 9
      i. Ethical Freedom 10
      ii. Psychological Determinism 10
   C. Hegel 10
      i. Historical Determinism 10
      ii. Ethical Freedom 11

III. WILL THIS SOLUTION WORK? 13
   A. The Scientific World-view 13
      i. External Coherence 13
      ii. Internal Coherence 14
      iii. Rationality 14
      iv. Responsibility 14
   B. Problem about Seriousness 14
      i. Genuine Culpability 14
      ii. Genuine Praise 15

IV. ANOTHER POSSIBILITY: INCOMPATIBILISM — 17
A. Epicurus — 17
   i. His Naturalistic World-View and Atheism — 17
   ii. Atomism — 17
   iii. The Atomic Swerve — 17
B. The Uncertainty Principle — 18
   i. Heisenberg's Discovery — 18
   ii. The Statistical Interpretation — 19
   iii. The London-Bauer Interpretation — 19
   iv. The Copenhagen Interpretation — 19

V. DEFECTS OF SECOND ALTERNATIVE — 21
A. Irrationality and The Uncertainty Principle — 21
   i. Heisenberg and Uncertainty — 21
   ii. Einstein's Reaction — 21
   iii. The Scientific, Deterministic World-View — 22
B. Scientific World-view — 22
   i. Determinism and Rationality — 22
   ii. External Coherence — 22

VI. PROMISE OF SECOND ALTERNATIVE — 23
A. Serious Solution — 23
   i. Moral Culpability — 23
   ii. Moral Praise — 23
   iii. Genuine Consistency with Moral World-View — 23
B. Milec Capek — 24
   i. Pathbreaking Book — 24
   ii. Radioactive Decay — 24
   iii. Indeterminacy in Nature — 25
   iv. Consistency with Science — 25
   v. Consistency with Rationality — 25

VII. IS INCOMPATIBILISM RATIONAL? — 27
A. Rationality and Common Sense — 27
   i. What is Common Sense? — 28
   ii. What is Rationality? — 29
   iii. Incompatibilism as Rational — 29
B. Rationality and Potentiality — 29
   i. Heisenberg and Potentiality — 29
   ii. The Concept of Potency — 29
   iii. Potency and Rationalism — 29
   iv. Potency and Empiricism — 29

VIII. THE SOLUTION OF KANT	31
A. Science and Religion	31
i. Back to Kant	31
ii. The Realm of Science	31
iii. The Realm of Religion	32
iv. Fichte's Interpretation of Kant's Noumena	33
B. The Bifurcation of the World	33
i. The Realm of Phenoumena	33
ii. The Realm of Noumena	33
IX. C.S. PEIRCE'S SOLUTION	35
A. Evolution of the Universe: From Tychism to Agappe	35
i. Tychism	36
ii. Agapism	36
iii. Synechism	37
B. Tychism and Rationality	37
i. Capek on Rationality	37
ii. How Tychism Fits the Definition	37
X. INCOMPATIBILISM, RATIONALITY, AND THE UNCERTAINTY PRINCIPLE	39
A. Incompatibilism and Potentiality	39
i. Potency and Capek's Criteria of Rationality	39
ii. Potency and Common Sense	39
iii. Potency and The Participation of the Observer	40
iv. Potency and Science	40
B. Incompatibilism and Things-in-Themselves	40
i. Mac Intyre's <u>Whose Reason? Which Rationality?</u>	40
ii. The Observer as Participant	40
iii. Scientific Limits of Knowledge	41
C. Incompatibilism and Tychism	41
i. The Participant in History	41
ii. Tychism and Incompatibilism	41
a. Rationality	41
b. Science	41
D. The Rational, Scientific, Holistic Nature of All Three Theories	41
i. What is Rationality?	41
ii. What is True Science?	41
iii. Rational Science as Holism.	42
iv. Conclusion: Freedom of Choice and Holism	42

Acknowledgments

In the entire production process for this book, several people must be singled out for special attention and gratitude: University Press of America and Mrs. Helen Hudson; the administration, philosophy faculty and students of both St. Joseph's University and Holy Family College; my mother and uncle. Last but not least, Mr. Thomas Mau of 69th St. Terminal Press, Upper Darby, PA for the outstanding typessetting.

CHAPTER ONE

THE PROBLEM OF FREE CHOICE

To begin with, why is free choice really a problem? It is patently obvious, is it not, that if an individual is confronted with two or more alternatives concerning a particular action or a particular profession in life, the intelligent individual can freely decide between them? What then is the problem of free choice?

The problem really begins when we consider the role of science in relation to free choice. Here again, you may claim that science has nothing to do with formulating a free choice either concerning an individual's life-work, a course of action or anything else. This may be true, and yet we may refer to what is often called the scientific worldview.

Now according to some, the scientific world view plainly provides enough data to prove that man is completely and totally a machine, no more endowed with free choice than is a computer. At best, man is a higher animal, and he is no more endowed with free choice than the higher animals, e.g., all primates, cats and dogs. According to many, science plainly reveals that the physical universe runs according to physical laws; man is also a physical being and he is a part of the physical universe; therefore, all of man's behavior must operate according to definite laws of psychology. When our knowledge is advanced enough, these laws will be able to predict all of our actions.

If all this is true, then man is not free; rather, he operates according to the laws of the machine, and he is no more free to choose than is a machine. This, according to some, is the scientific world-view. How do we know whether what some have described as the scientific world-view is correct or incorrect?

A. Free Choice and Science

Throughout the centuries, religion and philosophers have battled it out over the questions as to whether or not man has free choice. True, nothing else in the physical universe has free choice; but is man the exception? According to traditional Western religions, yes. But according to some philosophers, namely, those of a determinist persuasion, no. Let us review both positions slowly in order to determine who is correct.[1]

i. The Christian Tradition

Christians have always maintained that God, the Creator, has endowed man with free choice, either to serve God or to turn against Him. Here, free choice carries with it both reward and punishments. If one serves the Creator, the reward is the Beatific Vision, the sight of God for eternity after death. If the individual turns away from God throughout life, the punishment is hell, the loss of the Beatific Vision or the sight of God for all eternity.

ii. Augustine

It was Christian thought that inspired Augustine's treatise De Libero Arbitrio, or the Treatise on Free Will shortly after his conversion. The treatise was the solution to many of life's problems for Augustine, and his personal solution here was also the primary force behind his conversion.

How could an All-good God permit the existence of suffering in the world? When we look around, we see the suffering of innocent people; good people suffering from various diseases, people unjustly accused. Many, in the human race, had pondered problems of this sort for years before Augustine and one possible solution was Manicheanism—the belief in a good and in an evil Creator of the universe.

Manicheanism was a close descendant of the Persian religion of Zoroastrianism. In turn, Zoroastrianism was named after it's founder, Zoroaster, who made his living as a preacher. Now for many years, he was very unsuccessful and found few converts. In the end, however, Zoroaster was successful in converting many to his world view. According to Zoroaster, the world was ruled over by an all-good god, the god of light, and also by a god of evil. On the final day of the world, both of these powers would engage in battle and the god of light would win.

In a similar manner, the Manicheans believed that the world was ruled by the Prince of Light and the Prince of Darkness. Many of the members of this cult worshipped the Prince of Darkness. The evil which existed in the world, they attributed to the Prince of Darkness. Augustine in the fifth century, A.D., was one of their members.

But he was not convinced of the truth of Manicheanism. If the Prince of Light were all-powerful, how could he permit evil to exist in the world? Why could he not destroy the Prince of Darkness? It was questions like these which Augustine addressed to Faustus, the leader of the Manicheans, but he received no satisfactory answer. Could anyone answer Augustine's vexing problem?

Eventually Augustine met Ambrose, an intelligent and influential Christian at that time. He had previously thought that Christians could never number themselves among the thinkers of the world, but his meeting with Ambrose proved him wrong. Here was a Christian who was truly impressive. Because of Ambrose, Augustine became a convert to Christianity.

Christians had their own world view, distinct from Manicheanism. There was only one Almighty Lord of the universe, God. It is true that the Prince of Darkness or the Devil existed, but he was not Almighty. But why then did the Almighty Lord of the Universe permit evil?

Augustine's answer, in the De Libero Arbitrio, was that God created man with dignity and free will. Man had free will to lead a life of goodness and to turn toward

God or to lead a life of evil and so turn away from God. Hence, evil did not come from God. It came from man; man's free will. From the time of the writing of <u>De Libero Arbitrio</u> to the present, Augustine's stand has become equivalent to the position of Christianity on this issue.

iii. The Enlightenment

But is this position on free will something scientifically provable? Could it be, in any sense, made compatible with reason? Skipping ahead several centuries, this was a frequently asked question in the eighteenth century, the so-called Age of Enlightenment. It is a frequently asked question today. Can free will be reconciled with the picture of the universe we obtain from science?[2]

Science impressed eighteenth century man as it impresses many today. Science could always prove its points. It had demonstrated how the planets revolve around the sun and it had also demonstrated how blood flowed in the human body.

For the thinkers of the Enlightenment, the so-called philosophers, it had also demonstrated that man followed the physical laws of the universe to such a degree that he too was a physical machine. One of their number, La Mettrie, wrote a book with the title, <u>Man, the Machine</u>, and its object was just that, i.e., to prove that man is a machine.

iv. Determinism for Spinoza and Hobbes

In the century before the eighteenth, the seventeenth century, dubbed by historians as the Age of Reason, the philosophers, Spinoza and Hobbes had also tried to prove that free will did not exist; Hobbes in England and Spinoza on the Continent. For both philosophers, the notion of free will or free choice was an illusion.

Hobbes in England was what we would today call a "hard determinist", whereas Spinoza would amount to what we would today call a "soft determinist". For Hobbes, man was plainly not free and followed the laws of the machine; for Spinoza man was free in the sense that he could conquer his passions and lead his mind to the true "amor intellectualis Dei" or the true love of God. This is what today we would call ethical freedom. But similarly as for Hobbes, Spinoza would not grant any degree of true psychological freedom to man or rather, any genuine freedom to choose between alternatives.

v. Science vs. Religion

This was the problem. What religion plainly taught was plainly contradicted by science. Religion taught that man had true psychological freedom; real freedom of choice. But the philosophers of the Enlightenment as well as philosophers such as Hobbes and Spinoza thought that man was not free.

Who was right? Religion or science, as some interpreted science?

B. The Problem for Kant

This was also the dilemma of the philosopher, Kant, in the eighteenth century. He lived during the time of the Enlightenment, but he also had a religious upbringing.

4 WHAT IS FREEDOM OF CHOICE?

i. Pietistic Training in Gymnasium

Kant was born and raised in East Prussia, a region heavy with the revivalist spirit known as Pietism, then operative in Protestantism. Kant's mother was a devout Pietist. He seems to have remembered her quite well even into his old age.

ii. Enlightenment Training in University

The neighborhood pastor promoted Kant to university training at the city of Konigsburg, because he was good in his studies. At the University of Konigsburg, Kant became aware of most of the currents from the German Aufklarung, or Enlightenment, and later even wrote a well-known essay on it. Here, he was introduced by Martin Knutzen and others to the world of Isaac Newton and other famous scientists, and the philosophy of the Enlightenment.

iii. Either Science or Religion

Kant was torn between a religious and a scientific view of the world. Which world view should he adapt? Should he believe that man had free choice and could choose between right and wrong as his religion had taught or should he adapt the view of many followers of science that man was a machine?

iv. Why not Reconciliation?

Finally, would it be at all possible for Kant to adapt both of these points of view—science and religion? In other words, he would hold that both views of the world were correct, and that man was both free and determined. It would not be a matter of either—or. It would be a matter of both—and. In other words, it would be a true synthesis.

The only remaining problem was this. How could he have a true synthesis without contradicting himself?

v. Contradictions

How could man be both free and not free or, in other words, how could man be both free and determined? How could one make the world-view of both science and religion hold together, without having one side contradict the other?[3]

If what one side claimed about man was right, then what the other side claimed quite plainly had to be wrong. It was as simple as that. Or was it? Was there any logical matter of getting both sides to agree on this issue?

At first glance, it did not appear so. At first glance, this appeared to many of the intellectuals of the time to be one of those knotty issues which would bring about the downfall of religion. And this is what Kant at first thought.

But as time went on, what impressed Kant appeared to be that he began to think of science and religion as dealing with different realms altogether. If both science and religion treated different worlds altogether, then perhaps it would be possible to reconcile the two worlds. This was the project which inspired the whole rest of

Kant's philosophy.

The specific solution which Kant adapted for his unique philosophy, we will deal with in a later chapter. [Cf. ch. VIII - The Solution of Kant.]

[1] Sidney Hook (ed.), Determinism and Freedom.
[2] Corliss Lamont, Freedom of Choice Affirmed, Ch II.
[3] Corliss Lamont, op. cit., Ch V.

CHAPTER TWO

ONE POSSIBLE SOLUTION: COMPATIBILISM

Kant proposed one possible solution to the problem of free will, and exactly what he proposed is debatable even today. However, in the history of philosophy, many different theories concerning free will have been proposed. Most theories have been classified into one of two possible groupings: compatibilism and incompatibilism. We will discuss the merits and demerits of each of these types in turn. Let us begin with compatibilism.

As the compatibilists view the problem of free will, there is no real opposition between the theory that man is free and the scientific world-view that man follows definite, scientific laws of nature. The theory that man possesses free choice in his actions is know as Libertarianism. On the other hand, the theory that all of man's choices and activities are regulated by definite laws, and that man has no free choice is known as Determinism.

For the Compatibilists, there is no real opposition between Libertarians and Determinists. For the Compatibilists, it is totally possible that man follows definite laws of scientific behavior and that he is, nevertheless, a creature who freely chooses between right and wrong. Free choice and determination of that choice by definite, scientific causes are not incompatible. The individual may have chosen a particular course of action on the basis of definite causes, but this, by no means, implies that the individual in question lacked free choice in his actions. Therefore, Libertarianism and Determinism are compatible. In a similar manner, the stand of religion and the stand of science concerning man are totally compatible. This has always been the solution of the Compatibilist throughout history.[1]

A. Aristotle

In the almost universal opinion of scholars, Aristotle would be considered a Compatibilist. In the Physics, Aristotle considered that all living things operate under the laws of four causes: the efficient cause, the formal cause, the material cause, and the final cause. The efficient cause propels an object into motion. The formal cause constitutes the object as being what it is. The material cause specifies the kind of material or the kind of matter from which the object is made. The final cause is the most important cause of all. Final causality is the end or goal toward which the living thing develops; it is the purpose of the living thing. For example, the final cause of the acorn is to become an oak, and the final purpose of the child is to become a man (or woman).

In man, causality is operative, efficient, formal, material and final causes. But, most importantly, final causality is operative. Can any of this causality be reconciled with free will? In most interpretations of Aristotle, it could be and this is why Aristotle is often classified as a Compatibilist.

But where is the question of free choice discussed in Aristotle? Most commentators believe it is discussed in the Nichomachean Ethics and this comprises our next topic of discussion.

1. Knowledge and Action

According to Aristotle, in the Nichomachean Ethics, one could know very well the right course of action in a particular instance and yet not act upon this information. In other words, one could act in a manner completely contrary to one's best judgment. For many who have read the Nichomachean Ethics, Aristotle's statements concerning knowledge and action amount to a defense of free choice or free will. In other words, one could act contrary to one's best knowledge because the individual in question possesses free choice or free will. And it is probably true that Aristotle did hold to some version of free will.

But if Aristotle did indeed hold to a concept or belief in free will, did he ever think that both man's free choice and other contingent events in the universe ever violated the laws of causality in the universe: the laws of efficient, formal, material and final causes? It appears that he never thought so, for to have thought so would have been to violate his world view. Aristotle would not be Aristotle if he ever claimed that contingent events could take place without causes, or that man could choose between two or more alternatives on the basis of no causes whatsoever.

Aristotle was not an acausalist, and no one would ever claim that he was. For him, free will and causality operated together. Aristotle was a Compatibilist.

Then why did he claim that an individual could know the good and not do it? Is there a causal reason for this? This is the topic which we will next explore.

a. Knowing the Good

For Aristotle, one knows in general the ends of man. The good for man is evident to all men. The Real Good will promote man's true end. Man is naturally drawn toward the Real Good. The achievement of the Real Good will lead toward man's Happiness, or long-term satisfaction. This long-term achievement, whatever it may be, will satisfy man's rational nature.

Man knows the Real Good. He also knows the Apparent Good, what appears to be good at the moment. Often, this is not synonymous with the Real Good and operates against the achievement of the Real Good or of long-term goals. For example, many kinds of pleasure constitute the Apparent Good, what appears to be good for the individual now. The pleasure of drink, when done to excess, has often militated against long-range goals such as a happy family life.

Man knows the Real Good and the Apparent Good; yet he often chooses the Apparent Good. Why?

b. Doing it

ONE POSSIBLE SOLUTION: COMPATIBILISM

Aristotle recognizes that knowing the good is not doing it. Man may know the Real Good and yet choose the Apparent Good. Here, he will act contrary to his knowledge or better judgment. Is there a reason for this? Is there a cause?

Aristotle will never claim that there is no reason for this; that there is no true cause. Remember that we consider him to be a true compatibilist. Why then will someone choose the lesser or the worse cause? What is the reason for it? Aristotle states that the real reason, weakness of will.

What exactly is weakness of will? We will now explore this definite cause of human choice.

ii. The Major and Minor Premises

We will consider a specific example.

One drink too many will leave one inebriated. This drink is one too many.

∴ This drink will leave one inebriated.

The laws of logic would force an individual, who accepted both premises in this argument, to also accept the conclusion. But the individual might know the laws of logic and yet operate in a contrary manner. Why is this?

a. The Major Premise

The Major Premise causes no problems to speak of. Everyone knows, in the case of this particular example, that "One drink too many will leave one inebriated. "Our knowledge of the major premise, in this case and in many other cases, is firm.

b. The Minor Premise

In this and in all such cases, it is the Minor Premise which causes problems. One can be ignorant of the minor premise. One might know the major premise that "One drink too many will leave one inebriated, but not the minor premise that "this drink is one too many." For this reason, one will never conclude that "this drink will leave one inebriated."

Aristotle held that one could know what is right and yet not do because of weakness of will. But is there a reason for this weakness of will? Or, in other words, does this weakness of will have a cause? It appears that there is a cause for this "weakness of will" and that the cause amounts to a lack of knowledge of the minor premise. One does not know that "This drink is one too many" although one is quite aware of the major premise that "One drink too many will leave one inebriated but the cause of "weakness of will" is a lack of knowledge.

One neither acts nor, in this case, fails to act, without a reason, without a cause. Even when one knows something and acts otherwise, ignorance of the minor premise is the cause. Aristotle is thus a consistent Compatibilist. For him, Freedom and Causality do not contradict one another. Both are consistent or compatible.

B. Spinoza

Benedict Spinoza, in the seventeenth century, based his major work, the <u>Ethics,</u>

on the theory of Determinism, or the belief that psychological freedom, freedom of choice, is an impossibility. Reality, for Spinoza, was the one being "existing in itself and conceived through itself". This was the only true Substance. Its existence was Necessary. So, for that matter, was the existence of its modes. The modes of Substance were infinite and two of these were Space and Time. We exist in the modes of Space and Time; therefore, we are somehow Necessary.

It follows that all our behavior is somehow Necessary. All of our behavior is the result of definite causes. It makes little sense to attach any praise or blame to our activities. Spinoza stated that to understand was to forgive.

i. Ethical Freedom

Man, nevertheless, was free, in Spinoza's opinion. This meant that he was ethically free to remove himself from the bondage of the passions, "Human Bondage", in Spinoza's words. "Human Freedom", for Spinoza, consisted of the ability to control desire to the extent that one lived for the intellectual love of God, the "amor intellectualis Dei".

ii. Psychological Determinism

It was in the above-mentioned ethical sense, and in the ethical sense alone, that man was free. Man was not free, in the psychological sense, for Spinoza. He did not possess the ability for true free choice between alternatives. It was here that he was governed by necessity. Not to praise or blame, but to understand, was Spinoza's motto.

C. Hegel

Writing in the nineteenth century, the German philosopher Hegel claimed that history moved forward by the force of necessity. Great men, Hegel thought, were mere ripples in the surrounding social forces of history. The great man comprehends the peculiar Spirit of the Age, the Zeitgeist.

This was his claim to greatness. But he did not move history forward through his own free choice. Psychological freedom, or genuine freedom of choice was an impossibility for Hegel as it had been for Spinoza. But ethical freedom did exist for Hegel in the process of history, as it did for Spinoza in the human individual.

i. Historical Determinism

The Philosophy of Right, written in 1821, was the last book of Hegel's to appear in his lifetime. He would die ten years later, and his remaining works would be edited by his disciples, who would carry his work forward. Hegel would leave to the world a new sense of history—a sense of history as a pattern, an interconnected whole. Truth, according to Hegel, manifested itself in history. The Philosophy of Right addresses itself to the problem of history, but history is more clearly the focus of attention in Hegel's posthumous Philosophy of History.

The Philosophy of History is the story of the growth and development of Freedom from ancient times to the present, as Hegel saw it. In the ancient world of the despot, the Oriental World, only One was free. In the world of ancient Greece, the few, the aristocrats, were free. In the modern German world, strangely enough a monarchy, all are free.

ii. Ethical Freedom

Whether one agrees with some, all, or none of Hegel's descriptions becomes irrelevant to us at this point and to the issues with which we are dealing—the gradual growth and development of the concept of Freedom in history. For Hegel, the Spirit of the Age, the Zeitgeist, would determine the form of Freedom appropriate to that Age, and the individual, to exhibit some sense of genius, should be in touch with the Spirit of the Age. This was the sense of Freedom for Hegel. It consisted of being in touch with a moment of history, of being in tune with the Zeitgeist.

It was an ethical form of Freedom. But the movement of history itself exhibited a historical form of determinism. Great men did not constitute the moment in history by their own free choice. They simply reflected the Spirit of the Age in their historical function as geniuses. But they did not cause anything to happen. Rather, they were determined by the Spirit of the Age.

The development of the concept of Freedom throughout history was historically determined, according to Hegel. But if the individual were in touch with the Spirit of the Age and exhibited true genius, this individual was ethically free for he now reflected all the highly developed ideas of his own time. For Hegel as for Spinoza, ethical freedom existed because this was compatible with causation.[2] But, as for Spinoza, there was no psychological freedom, or freedom of choice because this was not compatible with causation. Both Hegel and Spinoza were, therefore, Compatibilists.

[1]Corliss Lamont, Ibid.
[2]Corliss Lamont, Freedom of Choice Affirmed, Ch. III.

CHAPTER THREE

WILL THIS SOLUTION WORK?

Aristotle, Spinoza, and Hegel have all been Compatibilists. All three of them have thought that Free Will and Causality do not contradict one another. All three have thought that an individual is responsible for his actions even if specific cause could be assigned for each of these actions.

In more modern terms, we might claim that an individual's personality is shaped by heredity and environment. These operate as causal factors influencing the personality of the individual. True, all of an individual's actions might be the result of that individual's heredity and environment. An individual's entire personality might be caused by his or her environment. But this does not mean that the individual in question is not responsible for his actions. Free will and responsibility are compatible, in the same manner as free will and causality are compatible. The individual is responsible for his own personality whether that personality is the effect of causes or not.

The theory of Compatibilism appears to have no problems connected with it, either for science or for religion. Both the free will accepted by most religions and scientific causality are accepted. Compatibilism appears to be wholly coherent with the scientific world-view. But a problem does arise which we will see later; namely, can we accept it in all seriousness?

A. The Scientific World-View

One reason for taking the theory of Compatibilism seriously is its evident coherence with the more established scientific view of the world. Many scientists, even today will probably accept some version of the scientist-philosopher Laplace, living in the eighteenth century. Laplace thought that if we ever knew enough about the physical laws of the universe, we could predict its future and the future of every individual in it. The only reason we cannot do this at present amounts to our own ignorance.

This is universal Determinism. Does Compatibilism fit in very well with this World-View?

i. External Coherence

As a theory, does Compatibilism have external coherence with Determinism? External coherence implies the ability to fit together with something outside itself, i.e., another theory, preferably a broader theory. Now Determinism is the broadest theory possible, applying to the entire universe, man included. Compatibilism, as a theory is much narrower, applying only to man and his free choice. We might consider it as a special case or a special application of Determinism.

As a special case, as a special application, does it fit in very well with Determinism? Certainly, nothing in either theory appears to contradict the other, for both theories, both the broad, universal theory and the special application are based upon Causality. Neither theory contradicts the causal view of the Universe.

So how can we claim that one theory is not coherent with the other? The narrower theory of Compatibilism, which applies simply to man, is externally coherent with the broader theory of Determinism, which applies to the entire universe. On external grounds, Compatibilism fits in with the scientific world-view.

ii. Internal Coherence

Also, the theory of Compatibilism could probably withstand charges that it is internally contradictory, or, we might say, self-contradictory. Philosophers such as Aristotle, Spinoza, and Hegel would probably maintain that there is nothing inherently contradictory in the concept that an individual can act as a free and responsible agent, and yet act as a result of specific causes influencing one's behavior. If we accept their conception of free choice, how can we prove them wrong? It appears that the theory of Compatibilism is internally coherent as well as externally coherent.

iii. Rationality

But is it rational? The question which arises here traces itself to Alisdair MacIntyre's Whose Reason? Which Rationality?. What model of rationality are we talking about? Whose rationality are we talking about?

If by rationality we simply mean internal and external coherence, then the theory of Compatibilism is certainly rational. But is it the only possible rational theory of free will or free choice? The answer to the last question we will explore in another chapter. [Chapter IV]

iv. Responsibility

Can one be a Compatibilist and take seriously the notion of responsibility? We can be certain that the Compatibilists have no problem with this. Perhaps it is here that we can begin to disagree with them.

B. Problem about Seriousness

The Compatibilists are at least consistent. But one could claim that they do not take free choice seriously. This is the claim I would like to make here in some detail.

i. Genuine Culpability

No one freely chose his own heredity and environment. If heredity and environment are the sole operative factors influencing one's entire personality and mode of behavior, then one's behavior and personality are not a product of free choice. How can we genuinely blame an individual for following the laws of his character if he could not possibly do otherwise. How can we seriously speak of freedom in this case? How can we seriously speak of choice?

ii. Genuine Praise

The same situation prevails in regard to reward or praise. Why either reward or praise the individual who could not seriously have acted otherwise than he or she did? The individual in question was simply following the unalterable laws of heredity and environment and could not possibly change her personality if she wanted to. The theory of Compatibilism seems to reduce all notion of praise and blame to insignificance. Can such a theory be said to take free choice seriously?

It is the author's contention that it does not, and so perhaps we are left to cast around for another theory.

CHAPTER FOUR

ANOTHER POSSIBILITY: INCOMPATIBILISM

If, indeed, Compatibilism cannot be taken seriously, what are the remaining alternatives? Are there any other real choices? Let us assume that Free Choice and Causality cannot genuinely go together without contradiction. Let us assume that we cannot take both of these together with any seriousness. What alternatives do we have left?

There is one large remaining alternative. This would be to assume, for the purposes of argument, that Free Choice and Causality could by no means go together, i.e., that they were not compatible. This is the stand known as Incompatibilism, and it has been maintained by various thinkers throughout history.[1] In this chapter, we will take a look at two of them: Epicurus, in the ancient world, and Heisenberg in the modern world.

A. Epicurus

Epicurus philosophized in the third century B.C. He was one of the first philosophers to preach a form of ethical hedonism. Pleasure, albeit the refined pleasures, was the goal of life. Epicurus instructed his followers to forsake the life of ambition and to retreat to the countryside. Ambition would certainly stand in the way of pleasure. Pleasure itself again, could amount to the simple, refined pleasures of a glass of wine or of reading a good book.

Epicurus, at least during his lifetime, had a large following, and after his death, his philosophy, born in ancient Greece, retreated from the West and moved into the Eastern world.

i. His Naturalistic World-View and Atheism

Much of Epicurus philosophy or world-view seems to have been very naturalistic. The gods, according to Epicurus, either did not exist or would not intervene in human affairs. There was no point in worrying about death because, now we are alive and death or non-being does not exist for us. The reality of the future does not yet exist and so, is not a reality. Only life in the present matters. This alone is reality. We must live to enjoy it.

ii. Atomism

Reality, to a great extent, was determined. Very much like his distant predecessor, Democritus, Epicurus thought that reality was comprised of particles too small to be seen by the human eye and known as atoms. There were round atoms and smooth atoms and atoms for the human soul. All nature was comprised of atoms, and all of nature was divisible into atoms.

Atoms followed the laws of nature. They banged into one another and collided with each other. Their random motions made up everything which we knew. But their motions were determined by laws — the laws of nature.

iii. The Atomic Swerve

Into all this determinism by the laws of nature, Epicurus introduced an element of chance. Not everything was a result of the laws of nature. Unpredictably, and without any known reason, according to Epicurus, the atom would swerve. This is why not everything which happened in nature could be predicted. This phenomena in his philosophy became known as "the atomic swerve".

This element of novelty in Epicurus' philosophy attracts our attention very much. It is very important for our purposes. Suddenly, not everything in Nature is predictable. Suddenly, not everything in Nature has a cause. Now there is genuine randomness in Nature and no one is sure how it got there. Finally, events without causes.

Could there be free atoms in the brain of man which operate in this manner? Man is then free, because not all of his atoms follow natural, physical laws. Some of his behavior is literally without a cause.

Epicurus "atomic swerve" could easily be classified as an early form of Incompatibilism. Causality and freedom are not compatible, but Freedom exists because some events, such as the "atomic swerve" are causeless. We have already seen how we can apply this form of Incompatibilism to man himself. Perhaps some of man's behavior is traceable to events without causes. Perhaps there is an element in Nature which is unpredictable. Perhaps. But can we prove this? If we could, then at last we could take free choice seriously. Incompatibilism seems to be a much more serious theory.

B. The Uncertainty Principle

If proof is what is desire, then Heisenberg's Uncertainty Principle may furnish it. There is some proof of a degree of unpredictability in Nature, and Heisenberg discovered this proof in 1931.

i. Heisenberg's Discovery

What troubled Heisenberg as a contemporary physicist was the enormous problem he and others were having with photographic plates of subatomic particles. Especially plates tracing the tracks of the very small subatomic particle, the electron. It seemed to be impossible to trace both the position and the velocity or, more accurately speaking, the momentum, of the electron. The more accurately one predicted the position of the electron, the more one seemed to have trouble predicting the velocity or momentum of the electron.

And vice versa. The more accurately one predicted the velocity or momentum of the electron, the more trouble one seemed to have predicting its position. One could predict one or the other, but not both. At first, many thought that when the scientific technology of making such measurements were perfected, then there would be no more problem. Total accuracy in predicting both position and momentum of the electron would be achieved.

But such perfection was not forthcoming. Were scientific instruments to

ANOTHER POSSIBILITY: INCOMPATIBILISM

blame? Most scientists in Heisenberg's time thought so, and so did Heisenberg. At least at first. But as time went on, Heisenberg changed his mind.

Maybe, thought Heisenberg, just maybe, our scientific instruments are not at fault and no matter how much we try to perfect them, we will do not better than we have done at present. Possibly it is Nature herself who is the unpredictable one. There may be an element of Uncertainty in Nature herself.

This thinking was at odds with all scientific orthodoxy. Most scientists of the nineteenth century, and also of the twentieth century, up until 1931, and for some time afterward, thought that Nature was strictly Determined. Some still think so.

But Heisenberg thought he could explain the path of the electron much better if he adopted the hypothesis of an element of unpredictability in nature. Heisenberg's bold claim was that not everything in Nature could be predicted.

ii. The Statistical Interpretation

The phenomena of subatomic particles covered by the Uncertainty Principle are unquestionable. It became evident to many scientists, after a while, that the Uncertainty Principle could "save the appearances". But how was one supposed to interpret the Uncertainty Principle itself?

One safe, conservative interpretation amounted to the stand that, in the realm of subatomic particles, one was usually dealing with a mass of particles, rarely with the individual particle. One could safely predict the behavior of the mass, because the conglomerate followed causal laws. It was the behavior of the individual particle which was difficult to predict.

For example, one could safely predict that a given mass of uranium, a radioactive element, would decay into half its original mass within a given period of time. This phenomena could be predicted because, in these cases, causal laws applied. Which particular uranium atoms would disintegrate it was nearly impossible to predict. But only because of our ignorance. Nature still followed causal laws but we did not yet know all of them. In the future, we would.

The Uncertainty Principle was hence a good methodological tool, but it did not tell us the truth about Nature. In the statistical mass, Nature was still predictable, and it still followed causal laws.

iii. The London-Bauer Interpretation

In this less safe and less conservative interpretation, Nature does not follow definite causal laws and is, in fact, always indeterminate until we observe it. Our observation of the electron changes its motion and position. We can never observe Nature in a neutral manner because we are always participants in Nature. We change it by our observations.

Our traditional scientific world-view that we are neutral observers of a causal universe must change.

iv. The Copenhagen Interpretation

To a great extent, this interpretation has already been discussed. In his book,

Physics and Philosophy, Heisenberg elaborates upon his conception of the universe.[2] The Copenhagen Interpretation is his interpretation of the universe.

Nature contains within it a degree of indeterminacy or possibility or potential. Aristotle called this principle in Nature, Potency. According to Heisenberg, it is time that we revived the Aristotlelian concept of Potency in our philosophy of Nature. Heisenberg re-interprets Potency, probably against the real causal philosophy of Aristotle, as the realm of the indeterminate and the acausal. Whether or not it is really Aristotle, this is nevertheless an interesting idea or interpretation of Potency.

Could Potency be the new indeterminate element in Nature? Perhaps we should take it into account in our philosophy of Nature, for we have for too long ignored it. By our observation of the electron, we change Potency into a definite position or velocity. In Heisenberg's interpretation of Aristotle, we hereby change Potency into Act.

[1]Corliss Lamont, Freedom of Choice Affirmed, Ch. II.
[2]Werner Heisenberg, Physics and Philosoophy.

CHAPTER 5

DEFECTS OF SECOND ALTERNATIVE

At this point, it might appear that the theory that both man and Nature contain an element of acausal indeterminacy may appear to be without blemish. Free choice becomes tenable because man's behavior is not completely an expression of causal laws. Acausality is real. And it follows from this that Incompatibilism makes sense.

Incompatibilism does have its critics, however. For that matter, the Copenhagen Interpretation of the Indeterminacy Principle is widely criticized, even today. "Is either theory truly rational?", the critics will ask. Is it really possible that Nature could ever operate without causes? Does the Copenhagen Interpretation of the Indeterminacy Principle fly in the face of everything we know or think we know about science? Namely, that it is rational to hold that all events in Nature have causes, and that, hence all events in Nature could be predicted. It is simply a matter of improving our technology up to that point.

A. Irrationality and the Uncertainty Principle

Perhaps the Uncertainty Principle is nothing but a blueprint for Irrationality. Some scientists have always suspected this, and for this reason, have taken the safe, conservative, statistical interpretation of the Uncertainty Principle. In this matter, they do not deny the Uncertainty Principle which does account for appearances, but they interpret it in a safe, deterministic manner.

i. Heisenberg and Uncertainty

Heisenberg himself obviously took the radical interpretation of his own Uncertainty Principle. Real indeterminacy does exist in nature. In his <u>Physics and Philosophy</u>, real potentiality also exists in Nature. Heisenberg himself may have been radical in the 1930's, but not everyone agreed with him.

ii. Einstein's Reaction

Neils Bohr agreed with him and helped him formulate the Copenhagen Interpretation. Among those who did not agree, we can include none less that the illustrious Albert Einstein among their number. All through the 1920's and the 1930's, Einstein debated with Bohr and with Heisenberg on this question.

Einstein had recently achieved world fame as the formulator of the Special and General Theories of Relativity. But the new physical world to which Einstein addressed the scientific community was a deterministic world. Temporality might even operate backwards in Einstein's world, i.e., from future to past, but it was still a world in which the laws of Causality were valid. This was not the world of Bohr and Heisenberg. Their world was a world of Indeterminacy.

Einstein could not tolerate this and he said so. "God does not play dice with the world." For Einstein, a world dominated by the Uncertainty Principle would be an irrational world indeed. Until the end of his life, he opposed the Copenhagen Interpretation of the Uncertainty Principle and much of Quantum Mechanics with it. Quite a few scientists joined him in this protracted attempt to save the concept of Rationality in the scientific world.

iii. The Scientific, Deterministic World-View

This brings us again to the Statistical Interpretation of the Uncertainty Principle. If we claim that the principle of Causality as we know it is still preserved in predictions for the mass, the visible, non-atomic level of ordinary experience, then we preserve one of the cardinal tenets of nineteenth century thought. The Statistic Interpretation is at least externally coherent with the deterministic, causal picture of the world which was inherited from nineteenth century thought. Any other interpretation could very easily be considered as irrational. The label of irrationality was a serious defect in the Copenhagen Interpretation of the Uncertainty Principle.

B. Scientific World-View

In the nineteenth century scientific worldview, which really goes back to the seventeenth century [Isaac Newton's formulation of the Three Laws of Motion and the Law of Gravity] all effects had causes. To be rational was equivalent to making all of one's scientific theories cohere externally with the Deterministic view of the universe. Not to be rational would be to fail to do so.

i. Determinism and Rationality

What model of rationality should an individual follow in his research? Throughout a good part of the twentieth century, that is, until the Uncertainty Principle became more widely accepted, the Deterministic view of the universe was regarded in scientific quarters as the equivalent of rationality. In some quarters, it still is today.

ii. External Coherence

External Coherence, as George Gale stated in his Theory of Science, is the most important criteria of whether a new theory ever becomes accepted. For a long time, this was the major problem of the Indeterminacy Principle. It lacked external coherence with a wider vision of the universe. Until this problem could somehow be corrected, it would always have a large problem finding acceptance.

Until it cohered with the wider vision of the universe, some would always claim that the Indeterminacy Principle was irrational. Eventually, scientists began to accept the world view of an indeterminate universe without causality as we know it. Then and only then, acceptance of the Copenhagen Interpretation of the Indeterminacy Principle begin to appear rational.

Is the Copenhagen Interpretation rational? If so, what is our picture of rationality? These questions will constitute the subject of our next chapter.

CHAPTER SIX

PROMISE OF THE SECOND ALTERNATIVE

Let us retreat back to Compatibilism for a moment. Can we consider Compatibilism a rational theory of man's behavior? We might say that it is, if it is only externally coherent with the way the universe is. Is the universe a causal universe or is it ultimately acausal? Is the Principle of Indeterminacy an explanation of the ultimate workings of the universe or not?

Milec Capek, along with many other philosophers of science and scientists, defend the Principle of Indeterminacy as ultimately explanatory of the nature of the universe. We will describe his thinking in this chapter. If he is right, then the theory of Incompatibilism is externally coherent with a universe in which the deterministic theory of the world is no longer
viable.

Also, the theory of Incompatibilism enables one to take the theory of free choice or free will seriously in a way in which the theory of Compatibilism does not. It is this latter point which we would like to discuss first, and then we will return to the Indeterminist view of the world held by Milec Capek.

A. Serious Solution

If Incompatibilism is right, and we cannot be sure at this moment that it is, we finally have a serious theory of free choice or of free will. No longer will it be necessary to claim that Free Choice and Causality operate together, and that one does not contradict the other. If there is a genuine degree of Unpredictability in Nature, this will enable us to take Free Choice seriously. It will enable us to deal more consistently with moral culpability and with moral praise.

i. Moral Culpability

No longer are individuals culpable simply because they follow the laws of their own heredity and environment. Now the individual is guilty because of genuine act of Free Choice. Psychologically, one is capable of confronting alternatives and of genuinely choosing between them because one is no longer bound by the laws of Causality. One can make a genuinely unpredictable choice and be morally culpable.

ii. Moral Praise

Likewise, the genuinely unpredictable choice can lead to moral praise. Here also, one is no longer bound by the laws of heredity and environment, or strictly determined to act in a particular manner. We can genuinely praise, for example, an individual who has overcome a particular type of hardship.

iii. Genuine Consistency with Moral World-View

But the largest advantage to be obtained from the theory of Incompatibilism is that it is totally consistent with the moral view of the world. The theory of

WHAT IS FREEDOM OF CHOICE?

Incompatibilism is not restricted by a Deterministic view of the world, a view of the world in which explanation must always be made in terms of causes. The acausal worldview, on which Incompatibilism rests, is much more in line with morality and genuine free choice than it is with science. The reason for this is that the acausal universe will permit real unpredictability at times, and the causal universe will not. Moral Free Choice requires some degree of unpredictability. If we can scientifically predict all moral free choice, where is the element of real Freedom?

B. Milec Capek

Milec Capek was a real pioneer in the area of the philosophy of science. It was he who interpreted the Indeterminacy Theory in a realistic fashion. Indeterminacy was a real feature of the physical universe for him, and not simply a product of our ignorance concerning real causes or our lack of a more developed scientific technology. Capek's interpretation would place the Indeterminacy Principle or the Uncertainty Principle on a scientific footing. A natural result of this, for our purposes is that it would also place the theory of Incompatibilism on a scientific footing as well as a moral footing. In addition Capek also thought that his interpretation of the Uncertainty Principle in quantum mechanics was completely consistent with all of our notions of rationality. We will discuss Capek's views in this matter also in the present chapter.

i. Pathbreaking Book

In 1961, Milec Capek published The Philosophical Impact of Contemporary Physics. It was a trailblazing work, which defended a realistic interpretation of the Uncertainty Principle. It would be impossible, in the author's view, to maintain a simplistic view of causality in the twentieth century. For Capek, both Quantum Mechanics and Relativity Theory together had revealed that space, time, motion, matter and causality were not completely distinct one from another but were interdependent, one upon another. Causality itself was much more difficult to understand as a result of this newer interpretation. Evidently, no one could any longer think of causality in simplistic nineteenth century terms.

ii. Radioactive Decay

The presence of radioactive decay established the truth of The Uncertainty Principle or of The Indeterminacy Principle in Capek's mind. The rate of radioactive decay did not depend upon the participation of the observer; the radioactive element would decay at a very steady rate, very much independent of whatever the observer thought or did.

When one had to consider particular atoms, no scientist could predict which particular atoms would decay, and one could only predict for the mass of atoms. But the randomness of radioactive decay indicated, for Capek, a randomness which took place independently of the human observer. There was a genuine randomness or unpredictability in Nature.

iii. Indeterminacy in Nature

For Capek, Causality, as we have seen, was not the simple Causality of nineteenth century science. Causality was very much interrelated with and interdependent upon space, time, motion, and matter. Space, time, motion, matter, and causality did not exist in watertight compartment, i.e., in complete separation one from another. For this reason, Nature was truly indeterminate. It did not follow the simple, causal rules of nineteenth century science.

iv. Consistency with Science

The larger problem for us is this. Can the Uncertainty Principle be made compatible with science? Capek things that it can. Twentieth century science simply must learn to function with the concept of acausality, in Capek's opinion. It cannot return to the Determinism of the nineteenth century.

v. Consistency with Rationality

But by far the largest problem with which we will have to deal is this. Is the Uncertainty Principle consistent with Rationality? Does it make sense to maintain the view of an acausal universe? By implication, or by application, is Incompatibilism a rational theory for an individual to hold?

Capek certainly thinks that the Indeterminacy or Uncertainty Principle and the theory of an acausal universe both make sense. Is he correct in this? Searching for the answer to this question will be the topic of our next chapter.

CHAPTER SEVEN

IS INCOMPATIBILISM RATIONAL?

What is rationality? What are its major characteristics? Everything depends upon our definition of rationality, or rather upon our model, as Alisdair MacIntyre states in his book, Models of Rationality. For Capek, there is nothing irrational about the Uncertainty Principle or, for that matter about all of contemporary physics.

Is rationality the equivalent of common sense? If this is true, then there are many things which are rational without meeting the criteria of common sense. The fact that the earth is round and not flat is rational. But does this fact meet all the criteria of common sense? So it may well be with contemporary physics. It may well meet all the criteria of rationality, but not necessarily all the criteria of common sense. Common sense and reason are not one and the same.

Also, is the Aristotelian concept of Potency or of Potentiality truly a rational concept? It is not a concept which relates to anything which we can represent mathematically or which we can see. Is it rational? Both common sense and potentiality will be two concepts which we will analyze in this chapter, in connection with the concept of rationality.

A. Rationality and Common Sense

In Milec Capek's opinion in The Philosophical Impact of Contemporary Physics, the Uncertainty Principle is rational but it does not conform to our common sense. In our common sense intuition of things, we like to think we understand the true nature of space, time, motion, matter, and causality. We think of all five of these as completely separate entities.

Our common sense tells us that space, time, motion, and matter and causality have nothing to do with one another, that they are completely separate entities. But this is precisely where our common sense makes a mistake. Our common sense would have us think that the amount of time which passes has absolutely nothing to do with the rate of motion of a vehicle or with the acceleration of the same vehicle. But this is not always true.

It is only true, according to Albert Einstein, because we have become so accustomed to objects which move at an extremely slow rate of acceleration. With extremely high rates of acceleration, time itself slows down. This was part of the meaning of Einstein's Special Theory of Relativity. One might imagine an atomic powered rocket ship of the future, which becomes accelerated to speed approaching that of the fastest moving entity in the universe, light. Light travels at about 186,300 miles per second. If a spaceship of the future left the earth at these highly accelerated speeds for a period of three years and then returned to the earth, the travelers might even find that everyone on earth had aged thirty years. And if they traveled even

28 WHAT IS FREEDOM OF CHOICE?

closer to the speed of light they might find that time in earth had retarded even more. Two hundred years would have passed and everyone whom they knew on earth would have died.

This part of the Theory of Special Relativity is known as the Time Dilation Effect. What is implied by this theory is that time and motion are not independent entities. They are very much dependent one upon the other. Time depends upon motion.

Space and matter also depend upon motion. At extremely high rates of acceleration, at nine-tenths of the speed of light, a twelve inch ruler will become a six inch ruler. In this manner, as Capek explicates, space, time, motion, and matter are interdependent. All four of these are also interdependent upon and interrelated with causality.

It is true that Einstein fought many of the implications of quantum mechanics. But in this, Capek thinks that Einstein made a mistake. The implications of both Relativity Theory and Quantum Mechanics are the same, in Capek's view. Space, time, motion, matter and causality are interrelated and interdependent.

i. What is Common Sense?

Does this contradict common sense? Possibly. It does not represent what most of us think or experience. Does it contradict reason? Capek thinks not. One need not become a committed irrationalist in order to accept these propositions. All that one need maintain is that we can no longer visually picture the universe, the way nineteenth century Victorian scientists could picture the universe.

Nineteenth century Victorian scientists could easily imagine a universe of atoms, particles too small to be seen with the human eye or even with a microscope. The atoms made up everything we know, and they later formed the symbols of today's chemistry equations. The atoms constantly banged and collided, one with another. Everything which existed was, hence, composed of particles of matter in motion which took up space and which endured in time.

Nothing in the nineteenth century challenged the imagination according to Capek. Space, time, motion, matter, and causality were entirely separate, very much as we ordinarily imagine them to be. Nothing in nineteenth century science challenged our ordinary common sense ideas of them.

But twentieth century science does. In the science of the twentieth century, molded as it is by Relativity Theory and the Uncertainty Principle of Quantum Mechanics, our imagination is challenged indeed. Now we must think of space, time, motion, matter, and causality as interrelated and interdependent.

How can we imagine this? Capek tells us that we can't. At least not visually, as we could visually picture the atoms of nineteenth century science, banging and colliding in space. We must try to imagine twentieth century science, if at all possible, with auditory imagery. Imagine the notes of a melody. No one note is especially significant, but together all of the notes make music. In twentieth century science, everything is interconnected and interdependent; this challenges the imagination. Maybe it even challenges our ordinary common-sense manner of looking at things as separate entities.

Does twentieth century physics also, however, challenges the concept of rationality itself?

ii. What is Rationality?

Again, what is rationality? Is it necessarily tantamount to the assumptions of many nineteenth century Victorian scientists who held that space, time, motion, matter and causality were separate? Why should we, in the twentieth century think that whatever does not challenge the imagination, as the science of the nineteenth did not, is necessarily rational?

Why is it not rather possible to think that rationality is precisely that which does challenge the imagination? To begin to think of reality in more imaginative terms as notes in an interconnected melody — to begin to think of space, time, matter, motion, and causality as interconnected; is not this a superior concept of rationality? This appears to have been Capek's opinion in The Philosophical Impact of Contemporary Physics.

iii. Incompatibilism as Rational

If twentieth century science is rational, as Capek thinks it is, why not Incompatibilism? Incompatibilism is nothing but the application of the Uncertainty Principle to man himself. Basically, the theory of Incompatibilism has always cast around for support in science. Without the existence of twentieth century science, it would make no sense at all. Nevertheless, twentieth century science does exist, and, as we have proven, it is a rational science. Incompatibilism is simply a special case of it and therefore, it too is rational.

B. Rationality and Potentiality

Furthermore, is the concept of Potency, with which Heisenberg sought to ground the Uncertainty Principle, at all rational? As mentioned, it cannot be seen; it cannot be reduced to a mathematical equation. Can such a concept ever be considered rational?

i. Heisenberg and Potentiality

In Physics and Philosophy, Heisenberg called for a grounding of the Uncertainty Principle in the concept of Potency. Potentiality, for Aristotle, meant possibility or potentiality; i.e., the possibility or potentiality of an acorn's becoming an oak; the potentiality of a fertilized egg to become a mature human being.

We might consider the electron as a potential state of existence until it is observed; when observed by scientific instruments according to the tracks which it makes, it is now a definite particle. Employing Aristotelian vocabulary, the electron, upon observation, is now in Act. The Aristotelian concepts of Act and Potency could, in Heisenberg's opinion, explain the Uncertainty Principle.

ii. The Concept of Potency

Let us return once again to the concept of Potency. If Heisenberg is right, we can employ the concept of Potency to ground the Uncertainty Principle itself. Is the concept of Potency Rational? It cannot be seen; it cannot be reduced to a mathematical equation. This causes problems both for philosophic Rationalist and for philosophic Empiricists.

iii. Potency and Rationalism

Throughout history, the concept of Potency has created enormous difficulties for Rationalists. Descartes, Leibniz and Spinoza in the seventeenth century all seemed to dismiss the Aristotelian concept of Potency. They certainly never employed this concept in any of their writings. Perhaps this is because it may be difficult to think of the concept of Potency as a "clear and distinct idea", which is as clear as the concept of mathematics or of number.

iv. Potency and Empiricism

Also, throughout history, the Empiricists have rejected the concept of Potency. For the Empiricists, the concept of Potency was something which could never be seen. In the eighteenth century, philosophers Locke, Berkeley, and Hume appear to have dismissed the concept of Potency as a throwback to the days of the Schoolmen.

True, the concept of Potency is not a "clear and distinct idea." It is not reducible to mathematics. It is also true that the concept of Potency cannot be seen. Is it therefore irrational?

No. No more than the Uncertainty Principle is irrational. Like the Uncertainty Principle, which it grounds, according to Heisenberg, the concept of Potency relates to a world in which everything—space, time, motion, matter, and causality — are interrelated and interconnected. Our imaginations are challenged to grasp this new, interconnected world. But reason itself is not challenged; it is only called upon to perform its traditional task, now more than ever — the task of understanding and living in an interconnected, interdependent physical world.

CHAPTER EIGHT

THE SOLUTION OF KANT

One of the major problems with which Immanuel Kant grappled in his philosophical writings was the problem of free choice, or, in the more usual terminology, free will. We have already alluded to Kant's problem in the first chapter. In this chapter we will discuss Kant's solution to the problem in the context of some of his major works in philosophy.

A. Science and Religion

In the religious world view of most Western religions, it is held that man has the power of free choice, i.e., the power to choose between alternatives, the power to choose good from evil, and right from wrong. Often standing in opposition to this is what many consider to be a scientific view of the world, a view of the world as entirely determined by causal laws, i.e., the laws of heredity and environment and so precluding any element of free choice. This underlying theme has been much discussed in previous chapters.

i. Back to Kant

If the reader remembers, in the first chapter, it was explained how Kant was greatly perplexed by the problem of free choice. Should he accept the reality of free choice and keep himself in line with the religious views of his Pietisitic upbringing. This was Kant's dilemma. How did Kant resolve this dilemma?

ii. The Realm of Science

In both The Critique of Pure Reason and The Critique of Practical Reason, Kant did offer a way out of the dilemma. He did not abandon either the concept of free choice or the Enlightenment, scientific view of the world. He held on to both science and religion. But how was this possible? Science, in the minds of many, stood for a deterministic view of the world and religion stood for a concept of free will. How could he avoid contradicting himself?

The Critique of Pure Reason was Kant's solution. To employ a term of Whitehead, it was here that Kant bifurcated the world, or divided it into two. The world consisted of two realms; a realm of science and reason, and a realm of religion and free choice. The realm of speculative reason, Kant called the realm of things-for-us [Dinge-fur-uns] or the realm of Appearance. These were also known as the phenomena.

This was the world as it appeared to us, the world we know in space and time. Experimental science, the science of the great Isaac Newton, always dealt with objects which were located in the physical world, i.e., located in space and time. Space and time were not external realities; they related to the way in which the mind structures or organizes the external world. They were what Kant called the Forms of Intuition, innate structures through which we organized the world. Through these structures and through other structures, the Categories of the mind: Categories such as Unity, Plurality, Totality, Reality, Negation, Limitation, etc., we organized the world around us.

The Categories and the Forms of Intuition constituted the structures of the mind; they were like the mental sunglasses through which the mind saw the world. The Categories and the Forms of Intuition so structured the world that we did not perceive the world as it really was but simply as it appeared to us. We experienced the Appearances or the Phenomena, the things-for-us [Dinge-an-sich]. This was the realm of science and of Speculative Reason.

iii. The Realm of Religion

We did not know things as they really were, things in themselves [Dinge-an-sich]. These existed in a realm which was inaccessible to science. This realm, in Kant's terminology was the realm of noumena. This realm was inaccessible to both science and to Speculative Reason. Yet it was accessible, at least in most interpretations, to the realm of Practical Reason.

Through Practical Reason, according to Kant, we understood ethical truths. We understood the dignity and individuality of man in these ethical truths. We understand the Categorical Imperative, in one formulation, that one should always treat man as an end and never as a means, in another formulation, that we should act always in such a manner that our action should become a norm for all humanity.

The sphere of Practical Reason will deal with the realm of ethics. We might also treat religious questions according to the sphere of Practical Reason, in Kant's opinion. Questions concerning GOD, FREEDOM, and IMMORTALITY are more appropriately dealt with by Practical Reason than by Pure Speculative Reason.

Pure Speculative Reason will find no answers to these questions, because they are beyond the realm of science and the spatio-temporal world. But Practical Reason has the answers. One must postulate the existence of a Supreme Lawgiver in order to lead a moral life. In order to lead a moral life, man must be able to choose freely between good and evil. One cannot be an automaton. Therefore, FREEDOM or free choice or free will becomes necessary for the leading of a moral life. Practical Reason requires it. Finally, IMMORTALITY becomes a necessity because justice is not something which is a reality for most people in this life. But Practical Reason requires that the imbalance become redressed in an afterlife. Hence, IMMORTALITY.

In bifurcating the world into two realms; the realm of Phenomena and the realm of Noumena, Kant solved his problem concerning free choice. In the realm of phenomena, man was a machine and followed the laws of the machine, very much as science viewed man. This was the realm of Appearance, the way the world looked to us through the eyes or the categories of science. But this was not the way things were. This was not the realm of things-in-themselves. This was simply the way man

THE SOLUTION OF KANT

himself structured the world. Space and time itself did not belong to things but to man's mental structure.

But in the realm of noumena, the realm of things-in-themselves, man was free. In the realm of things as they are, man was free. He was free to choose right from wrong. He had free choice or free will.

Free choice or free will was real, but science could never prove it. Science had inbuilt limitations. It dealt only with the physical world of space and time. It did not deal with what lay beyond those limitations. But Practical Reason did. It dealt with the noumena, with things as they are in themselves. Practical Reason dealt with GOD, FREEDOM, and IMMORTALITY. Practical Reason dealt with Free Choice even if science and Speculative Reason couldn't because of the question of Free Choice was out of the area of its competency.

iv. Fichte's Interpretation of Kant's Noumena

After Kant's death, his Critique of Practical Reason became the starting point of a younger German philosopher, Johann Gottlieb Fichte, who died in 1814. Fichte thought that reality itself was a matter of imposing our moral law on Nature.

This, in Fichte's philosophy was the realm of noumena.

Nevertheless, Fichte took objection to Kant's concept of the noumena. If noumena are inaccessible to Speculative Reason, then, as Kant himself admitted, we can never know the existence of the noumena through pure, Speculative Reason, then how do we ever know that they exist?

For Fichte, we don't, unless we later claim that we know the existence of noumena through intuition. Through intuition, according to Fichte, we know that free will exists, and this is the realm of man's direct access to the noumena. We know that free choice or free will exists because we can experience our own freedom. All later German Idealist Philosophers went on to deny the existence of noumena, because all experience was somehow accessible to man.

B. The Bifurcation of the World

What did Kant accomplish concerning free choice or free will through his bifurcation of the world? This is the topic with which we would presently like to deal.

i. The Realm of Phenomena

The realm of phenomena is the realm of Appearance. It is the realm of Speculative Reason and of science. Science deals with Appearances only, whether in regard to man or in regard to anything else. Its limitations are that it deals merely with the spatio-temporal world, and with nothing which lies beyond.

ii. The Realm of Noumena

The realm of Noumena relates to the realm of thing-in-themselves. It is the realm of Practical Reason and of religion. It is also the realm of man's Free Choice, of which we can have a direct intuition, according to Fichte.

What kind of freedom is he speaking of in the realm of noumena and of Practical Reason? It is definitely the psychological freedom of choice between right and wrong, in which Kant is interested. Do these choices have a cause in one's heredity and environment or not? In other words, the question we are asking here is whether Kant is a Compatibilist or not so. Is he an Incompatibilist? Does he think that the Free Choice or Free Will operates without causes.

It will be my thesis that Kant is an Incompatibilist. The reader must remember that we are dealing here with the realm of noumena or thing-in-themselves. Noumena, in Kant's philosophy are beyond the realm of Causality. Causality, for Kant, is one of the Categories of the human mind through which we structure the world. In other words, Causality is in the mind.

The realm of things-in-themselves, the realm of noumena, on the other hand, are not in the mind at all. This realm is decidedly an acausal realm. Man makes decisions in this realm of Practical Reason, according to Fichte's interpretation of Kant, which appears to be more than simply plausible. Hence, he makes these decisions in an acausal realm of experience which is inaccessible to pure, speculative reason.

These decisions in the noumenal realm are not based on causes. Kant was plainly an Incompatibilist. And perhaps he is right. Perhaps this is the solution to the problem of Free Choice or Free Will. But we will return to this in the last chapter. Now, in the next chapter, we must investigate the meaning of freedom for another famous philosopher who treated this question. We will examine the tychism of Charles Sanders Peirce, and ask ourselves whether this amounts to another version of Incompatibilism or not.

CHAPTER NINE

CHARLES SANDERS PEIRCE'S SOLUTION

Charles Sanders Peirce, who died in 1914, is a very well known figure in American philosophy. He certainly ranks with William James and John Dewey as a foremost leader of the Pragmatist movement in philosophy, which stressed that the criteria of truth is in consequences. A successful consequence might be the guarantee of the truth of a particular concept or belief.

Peirce wanted himself to be known as a Pragmaticist rather than a Pragmatist. This ugly-sounding name might, he thought, distinguish his beliefs sufficiently from Pragmatism. He believed that the truth of any particular concept was to be found in its consequences, but not the subjective consequences of holding to a belief which was satisfying. Peirce thought of truth as that result upon which science would converge at the end of its ideal research. At this point, we would all know the results upon which science would converge — we would all know the final consequences.

At any rate, we will not dwell upon Peirce's Pragmaticism in this chapter but rather upon one of the bold, speculative essays which he wrote in Milford, Pennsylvania, in his retirement from the Geodetic Survey toward the end of his life. Peirce was not a teaching professor, although he had taught previously for five years at Harvard. Throughout life, he developed a drinking problem.

Let us consider, however, his essay on "Evolutionary Love". It is this essay which ties in very much with the theory of Incompatibilism for our present purposes. The essay of "Evolutionary Love" traces the three stages of love and life throughout the history of man. It embraces his past, his present, and his future.

Was Peirce a Compatibilist or an Incompatibilist in regard to the question of Free Choice or of Free Will? It appears that Peirce was an Incompatibilist on this essay, and it is the point of this chapter to prove that this is the case. I intend to use the essay, "Evolutionary Love", as a fulcrum or reference point for this discussion. It represents Peirce's clearest statement in regard to the problem of Free Choice or of Free Will.

A. Evolution of the Universe: From Tychism to Agappe

In the opinion of C.S. Peirce we might trace the history of the universe and discover that it is evolving toward a definite goal. What is the goal? Greater technological mastery of the world or, perhaps, the universe? Greater scientific knowhow? Greater knowledge of science? Or perhaps the goal of history is an extension of democratic equality to more and more people, or the granting of human rights to everyone. Perhaps it is greater economic equality. For C.S. Peirce, all of these greater goals could be embraced under a much broader umbrella, i.e., the goal of increasingly greater order in the world or in the universe.

i. Tychism

Peirce speculates in his later essay that the first stage the universe underwent relates to its origins in the distant past. He calls this distant first stage of the universe the stage of tychism. In the tychistic universe, shortly after the origin of the universe itself, sheer Chaos prevails. All events take place randomly. No events take place under the rule of law, for in the stage of tychism, there is no natural laws of the universe. Everything which takes place here takes place according to chance. There are no lawlike events. This may very well be the stage of the universe in which the laws of Causality do not apply.

This could be the universe in which the Aristoteleian concept of Potency prevails. This could also, very easily be the universe of the Indeterminacy Principle. It is the acausal world of Potency or Potentiality to which Peirce seems to be alluding, even though he may not have been that well aware of Aristotle [of all the Pragmatists, however, Peirce seemed to be the only one who was aware of the Scholastic Philosophers]. It is his references to the tychistic universe that Peirce plainly reveals himself to be an Incompatibilist. His references to an acausal universe have definite applications to man and to the realm of Free Choice or of Free Will, as we will see in the sections below.

ii. Agapism

The second stage in the evolution of the universe relates to the present history of mankind. It is the stage which Peirce calls agapism. Spontaneity and chance still take place in this world, and they even prevail. Hence, this is still an acausal world, an indeterminate world of Potentiality.

There is much lawless behavior in things and in humans. Not everything operates according to plan. Some affairs take place by chance. There is nothing to regulate these acausal occurrences.

But lawlessness and spontaneity does not describe all of the events which take place in this world. There arise, in the world, for the first time, the appearances of some semblance of order in the world. Some events have definite causes. Definite laws of nature and definite patterns begin to appear. Certain patterns of human behavior become regulated, habitual, and more and more lawlike as time moves on. The growth of science and its applications in technology will hasten this process.

With the increasing growth of science and technology, we will begin to see more and more regulated and controlled human behavior following definite psychological and physical laws. The element of spontaneity and chance will begin to disappear.

Nevertheless, if we apply the present moment, the stage of agapism, to human behavior, we will find that human behavior contains an element of lawlike behavior and an element of acausal spontaneity. It is this element of acausal spontaneity which still enables us to speak of Incompatibilism, or of genuine, serious Free

Choice operating within human behavior without causes. The world view which Peirce presents in the stages of tychism and agapism enable us to speak of Free Choice and Incompatibilism. This is because real Free Choice and Incompatibilism demand the acausal universe which Peirce presents in the early stage of the universe's evolution, i.e., the stages of tychism and of agapism.

iii. Synechism

From the Greek word for true love, synechism represents for Peirce the future of mankind. As the future moves forward, the element of chance and acausality of the tychistic universe begins to disappear completely. The rule of law and harmony become predominant. Eventually, all human behavior becomes completely predictable and lawlike. All human behavior eventually becomes completely harmonious. All events will take place according to definite causes in the future evolution of the universe. Causality will triumph over acausality.

In the distant future of the human race, therefore, one might claim that Compatibilism will be the best explanation of Free Choice or Free Will. Then, we will be able to refer only to a causal universe, and not at all to an acausal one. But for the present world, the world of agapism, the spontaneity and acausality of at least some events seem to best fit in with the theory of Incompatibilism or of Free Choice not entirely based upon Causality.

B. Tychism and Rationality

Finally, is the universe depicted by Peirce in the tychistic phase of the evolution of the universe, a rational picture of the world? Evidently not, if one is Victorian in one's thinking and holds to a nineteenth century view of the world in which space, time, motion, matter and Causality are separate, one from another.

i. Capek on Rationality

On the other hand, it definitely is a rational picture of the universe if we preclude ourselves from such a view and move into the world of the twentieth century, the world of which Capek speaks when he claims that space, time, matter, motion and Causality are intercommected and interdependent entities. This is the acausal universe of Potentiality [a revival of an ancient Greek concept in the twentieth century, strangely enough] and of the Indeterminacy Principle. We cannot imagine this world as easily as Victorian man could imagine his nineteenth century world view because our world view in the twentieth century is more challenging. And yet we can conceive of such a world, a challenging, rational world indeed.

ii. How Tychism Fits the Definition

All of this seems very definitely to apply to thetychism of Charles Sanders Peirce. The tychistic universe in "Evolutionary Love" is a universe based on the features which we have mentioned in regard to our twentieth century concept of rationality: indeterminate, potential in some respects, and acausal. In this way, tychism fits the definition of rationality.

And the tychistic universe of Peirce, along with the *agapism* of the present, represents a universe in which real Free Choice, on the foundations of the theory of Incompatibilism, is possible. Peirce's *tychism* is similar to Kant's noumena in this regard. They both provide one with an acausal foundation for Free Choice, precisely the theory of Imcompatibilism.

CHAPTER TEN

INCOMPATIBILISM, RATIONALITY, AND THE UNCERTAINTY PRINCIPLE

It is time to try to tie together the remaining threads of our story. Both Aristotle's concept of Potency or of Potentiality, Kant's realm of noumena or of things-in-themselves, and Peirce's universe of tychism present for us many different ways of looking at the universe but they all share one trait or feature in common. All of these concepts present us with an acausal view of the universe, a view of the universe which, once again, could ground the theory of Incompatibilism. Are all of these views in line with science and with rationality We have already seen that they are.

But are all of the above-mentioned views inline with the science of the twentieth century? One again, our verdict is that they are. It is also the verdict of Milec Capek in The Philosophical Impact of Contemporary Physics. What exactly is the science of the twentieth century, if we were to explicate Capek's point of view, and exactly how does it differ from the science of the nineteenth century, in more explicate terms than we have considered up to this point? This will be our topic of discussion in this the tenth and concluding chapter of the book.

A. Incompatibilism and Potentiality

We have seen that Aristotle's conceptions of Potency and Act can be interpreted as a form of Incompatibilism even though Aristotle seems never to have rejected a completely causal picture of the universe. Heisenberg, in Physics and Philosophy has interpreted Potentiality in a completely acausal manner, has interpreted Potency in a completely acausal manner. We have seen that he can justify this interpretation of Potency. Is the concept of Potency rational, is it common sense, does it fit the definition of good science?

i. Potency and Capek's Criteria of Rationality

Capek's concept of rationality is the twentieth century concept of rationality: an interconnected, interdependent sense of rationality. This sense of rationality fits the concept of Potency or of Potentiality. One cannot know both position and momentum or acceleration of the electron with equal precision because matter and motion are interconnected, in Capek's opinion. This is also Heisenberg's interpretation of Potency — an indefinite particle with indefinite momentum. Both are indefinite, in Capek's opinion, because we cannot definitely separate one from another. But such a notion of separation is not at all a part of our contemporary notions of rationality. Unless we want to live once again in the nineteenth century Victorian world.

ii. Potency and Common Sense

Does the concept of Potency make common sense? Certainly, unless we think as our nineteenth century Victorian ancestors. Does not everything contain within it a principle of possibility? Every generation since Aristotle has known this, possibly even nineteenth century scientists with their concept of potential and kinetic energy.

iii. Potency and the Participation of the Observer

In Heisenberg's interpretation, the positon and momentum of the electron are indefinite until an observation is made. The observation is roughly equivalent to the participation of the observer. When the observation is made, Potency is reduced to something definite, to Act in the philosophy of Aristotle. This concept of Potency and Act could also fit the London-Bauer interpretation of the Uncertainty Principle, according to which the observer changes the nature of the electron which he or she observes.

iv. Potency and Science

There is nothing in twentieth century science which contradicts the concept of Potency. Space, time, motion, matter and causality are all interrelated and so indefinite in nature. The concept of Potency or Potentiality or Possibility is also indefinte in nature.

B. Incompatibilism and Things-in Themselves

Fichte thought that the realm of noumena or the realm of things-in-themselves was the realm of Free Choice or of Free Will. Noumena are beyond the causal world, for Causality was a category of the mind for Kant. In the acausal, noumenal realm, we have the grounds for the theory of Incompatibilism.

i. Mac Intyre's Models of Reason

Mac Intyre's new book was an eye opener for many. Upon reading it, many philosophers began to understand that there was not one model of reason but many. Reason does not have to pattern itself on the clear-cut demarcations of nineteenth century Victorian science. It could also model itself, or rather, be modelled on the twentieth century model of the interconnected, interdependent world.

Using this twentieth century model, the concept of Causality becomes indefinite for it becomes related to the concept of space, time, motion, and matter. Using this model, the traditional concept of Causality becomes both indefinite and acausal. This acausality provided good background for the theory of Incompatibilism. Finally, the acausality belongs to the realm of Kant's things-in-themselves, or to the realm of noumena.

ii. The Observer as Participant

What the observer observes is the realm of phenomena. This is the definite spatio-temporal world of the electron. One observes either the electron's position or the electron's momentum with accuracy. The realm of the indefinite position and the indefinite velocity, one could claim, belong to the realm of the Kantian noumena.

iii. Scientific Limits of Knowledge

The scientific limits of knowledge are what the observes sees. He sees the electron with either a definite position or a definite momentum. The indefinite, potential electron, we might say, is beyond the limits of human knowledge. It will never be known with scientific, speculative reason.

C. Incompatibilism and Tychism

At last, we come to Peirce's Tychism once again.

This concept provides an excellent foundation for Incompatibilism as well as the concept of Potentiality and the concept of Kantian things-in-themselves or noumena.

i. The Participant in History

Even in Peirce's conception of the evolution of the universe, it is the participant who makes possible the future world of synechism, or harmonious, regulated love. The participant makes the indefinite into something definite, very much in the same manner in which the observer makes the electron definite by observing it.

ii. Tychism and Incompatibilism

Finally, is tychism rational? Is it scientific? We have seen that by twentieth century standards it is.

a. Rationality

The conception of the acausal universe is sychronous with Capek's twentieth century concept of rationality.

b. Science

Again, acausality and science are compatible if one holds to the perfectly reasonable standards of science set forth in Capek's The Philosophical Impact of Contemporary Physics.

D. The Rational, Scientific, Holistic Nature of All Three Theories

One could base the theory of Incompatibilism on either an Aristoteliean notion of Potentiality or upon a realm of Kantian things-in-themselves or finally, upon Peirce's notion of a tychistic universe, which was supposed to have existed in the past. Whichever ground one chooses - Potentiality, Noumena, or Tychism, we have seen that all three theories are rational and scientific by twentieth century standards. In addition, all three of these concepts are holistic, i.e., they can ground a theory that space, time, motion, matter, and causality, are interconnected, interdependent, and indefinite. Again, all three theories can ground Incompatibilism.

i. What is Rationality?

All three theories — Potentiality, things-in-themselves, and Tychism are rational theories by twentieth century standards of rationality. All theories can be accomodated to a universe which is interconnected and interdependent.

ii. What is True Science?

The canons of true science will view space, time, matter, motion and causality as part of an interconnected, interdependent universe. The universe depicted in this manner is a holistic universe.

iii. Rational Science as Holism

Real, twentieth century science will view the world as an interconnected, interdependent whole —with space, time, motion, matter and causality as connected. What other choice is there? To go back to the pre-Relativistic and pre-Heisenburg, pre-Quantum Mechanics era of nineteenth century Victorian science?

iv. Conclusion: Freedom and Choice and Holism

Imagine, if you will, a holistic universe with space, time, motion, matter and causality as interlinked and interdependent one upon the other. Such a universe could accomodate many philosophic worldviews — the Aristotelian world-view of Potentiality, the Kantian world-view of things-in-themselves, together with Peirce's tychistic universe. In turn, as we have seen in some detail, all three of these worldviews are acausal and all three of them could accomodate the theory of Incompatibilism.

Incompatibilism is both scientific and rational in the modern, holistic, interconnected, interdependent sense of both science and rationality. As a theory, it has no real problems in being externally coherent with the scientific world-view, provided we hold to a truly contemporary version of that world view. In addition, the theory of Incompatibilism has one further advantage, namely that it is the only theory of Free Choice or Free Will which takes Free Choice, morality and the concepts of praise and blame seriously.

BIBLIOGRAPHY

Barret, William. Irrational Man: A Study in Existential Philosophy. New York: Anchor Books, 1962. One of the first books to introduce Existentialism to the United States. Read it to study the meaning of psychological freedom, or freedom of choice.

Bunge, Mario. The Place of the Causal Principle in Modern Science. Cleveland and New York: World, 1963.

Campbell, C.A. In Deference of Free Will, With Other Philosophical Essays. London: Allen & Unwin, 1967.

Capek, Milic. The Philosophical Impact of Contemporary Physics. Princeton: Van Nostrand, 1961.

Heisenberg, Werner. Physics and Philosophy: The Revolution in Modern Science. Introduction by F.S.C. Northrop. New York: Harper & Rowe, 1958. Re-introduced the concept of Potency into modern philosophy of science.

Hook, Sidney. (ed.) Determinism and Freedom in the Age of Modern Science. New York: Collier Macmillan Publishers, 1958. Presents the debate among modern scholars over whether man has freedom of choice.

Lamont, Corliss. Freedom of Choice Affirmed. New York: Horizon Press, 1969. In addition to other fine qualities, he anticipates very well the ensuing debate between Compatibilists and Incompatibilists.

Whitehead, Alfred North. Science and the Modern World. New York: The Free Press, 1953. Originally published, 1925. Presents very well the holistic implications of Quantum Mechanics and Relativity Theory.

Wild, John. Existence and the World of Freedom. Englewood Cliffs, N.J.: Prentice-Hall, n.d.

What Is
FREEDOM OF CHOICE?

Freedom of Choice is a sustained attempt to defend Incompatibilism, the position that a belief in free choice and a belief that every event has a cause are mutually contradictory positions. Using modern science's Uncertainty Principle as a foundation for evidence, Settanni avers that traditional concepts like causality must be abandoned, even on the Macro-Level, in the face of human unpredictability. The author reasons that only the Incompatibilist position takes the concept of free choice seriously, and argues against any causality that attempts to trace its origins to heredity or environment, as it negates the importance of human action.

Freedom of Choice is a persuasive, scientifically-based argument for taking free choice seriously. It is the only study in its field to examine in such detail the definition of rationality and to explain how Incompatibilism exhibits all the characteristic features of that philosophy.

Harry Settanni is a philosophy professor at St. Joseph's University and Holy Family College, both in Philadelphia. For the past fifteen years he has been a philosophy professor at various colleges and universities. He earned his Ph.D. from St. John's University in New York, his M.A. from Villanova University in Pennsylvania, and his B.S. from St. Joseph's University. Dr. Settanni has published three previous books with University Press of America:

What is Morality? Questions in Search of Answers
Five Philosophers: How Their Lives Influenced Their Thought
Scientific Knowledge: Discovery of Nature or Mental Construction?

ISBN 0-8191-8674-0